Why Can't I Learn Like Everyone Else?

Kids with Learning Disabilities

Kids with Special Needs

Why Can't I Learn Like Everyone Else?
Kids with Learning Disabilities

by Sheila Stewart and Camden Flath

MASON CREST PUBLISHERS INC.
370 Reed Road
Broomall, Pennsylvania 19008
(866)MCP-BOOK (toll free)
www.masoncrest.com

First Printing
9 8 7 6 5 4 3 2 1

ISBN (set) 978-1-4222-1727-6   ISBN (pbk set) 978-1-4222-1918-8

Library of Congress Cataloging-in-Publication Data

Stewart, Sheila, 1975–
  Why can't I learn like everyone else? : kids with learning disabilities / by Sheila Stewart and Camden Flath.
      p. cm.
  Includes bibliographical references and index.
  ISBN 978-1-4222-1726-9   ISBN (pbk) 978-1-4222-1929-4
  1. Learning disabled children—Education. 2. Learning disabilities—Treatment. I. Flath, Camden, 1987– II. Title.
  LC4704.S755 2010
  371.9—dc22
                           2010011420

Produced by Harding House Publishing Service, Inc.
www.hardinghousepages.com
Design by MK Bassett-Harvey.
Cover design by Torque Advertising Design.
Printed in the USA by Bang Printing.

Photo Credits
Creative Commons Attribution 2.0 Generic/Unported: Camazine pg. 34; mricon pg. 37; GNU Free Documentation License, Version 1.2 morgueFile: jdurham pg. 38; taliesin pg. 31; United States Air Force, United States Army: Ford, Kyle pg. 40.

The creators of this book have made every effort to provide accurate information, but it should not be used as a substitute for the help and services of trained professionals.

# *Introduction*

To the Teacher

Kids with Special Needs provides a unique forum for demystifying a wide variety of childhood medical and developmental disabilities. Written to captivate an elementary-level audience, the books bring to life the challenges and triumphs experienced by children with common chronic conditions such as hearing loss, intellectual disability, physical differences, and speech difficulties. The topics are addressed frankly through a blend of fiction and fact.

This series is particularly important today as the number of children with special needs is on the rise. Over the last two decades, advances in pediatric medical techniques have allowed children who have chronic illnesses and disabilities to live longer, more functional lives. At the same time, IDEA, a federal law, guarantees their rights to equal educational opportunities. As a result, these children represent an increasingly visible part of North American population in all aspects of daily life. Students are exposed to peers with special needs in their classrooms, through extracurricular activities, and in the community. Often, young people have misperceptions and unanswered questions about a child's disabilities—and more important, his or her abilities. Many times, there is no vehicle for talking about these complex issues in a comfortable manner.

This series will encourage further conversation about these issues. Most important, the series promotes a greater comfort for its readers as they live, play, and study side by side with these children who have medical and developmental differences—kids with special needs.

—*Dr. Carolyn Bridgemohan*
Boston Pediatric Hospital/Harvard Medical School

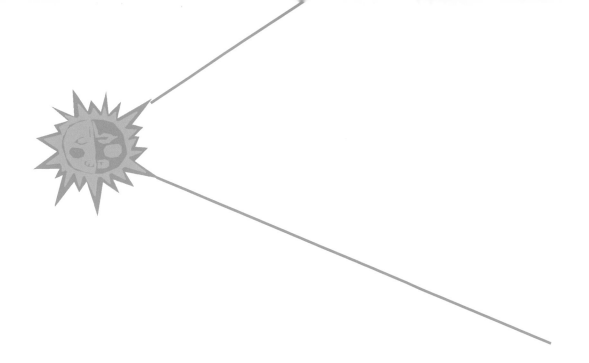

On Tuesday, there was a new girl
in class. She had long black hair
and a small face, and her name was
Mishti. Will thought she was beauti-
ful. Still, he didn't think about her
all that much until lunchtime, when
he overheard her talking to Delaney
and April.

"Well, I'm going to be an anthropologist when I grow up," the new girl was saying.

Delaney and April didn't seem to care about Mishti being an anthropologist.

"I love your shirt," Delaney said. "Where'd you get it?"

Will stopped listening and went to sit down with his friend Brandon.

"The new girl, Mishti, wants to be an anthropologist!" he told Brandon.

"So?" Brandon asked, chewing on his sandwich. "What's an anthropologist?"

"Anthropologists study people. Like where they come from and their cultures and stuff. *I* want to be an anthropologist too."

"You?" Brandon laughed. "Man, you can't even read."

Will glared at him. "Shut up. I can read." *Sort of,* he added to himself.

"Yeah, okay," said Brandon, "whatever." He rolled his eyes. "Maybe you should stick with something you're good at. You know, like playing the piano. You're pretty awesome at that."

"Not really." Will had been excited about Mishti liking anthropology—not too many fifth graders besides himself had even heard of it—but now he felt grouchy and discouraged. He *could* play the piano but only by ear, because he couldn't read the music. When he looked at the notes, they got just as scrambled in his brain as letters did.

At the end of the day, when everybody was getting their coats on, Will got up his nerve to talk to the new girl.

"Hey," he said. "I heard you say at lunch that you wanted to be an anthropologist."

"Yeah." Mishti looked at him, but she didn't say anything else.

"Um." Will felt himself start to blush. "That's cool. I want to be an anthropologist, too. My dad teaches anthropology at the university."

"Really?" Mishti looked a little interested now.

Then April came over and interrupted whatever she might have said next. "Just ignore him, Mishti," she said. "He's so stupid. He's lying about his dad, too. His dad owns a hardware store downtown."

"That's my stepdad!" Will said, but April was already pulling Mishti away.

"Just let it go," Brandon said from behind him. "Even if you and that new girl both care about the same weird thing, doesn't mean you're going to be best friends. Besides, I'm your best friend." He punched Will in the arm. "Hey, are we going skateboarding today?"

"Yeah, sure." Will did like skateboarding. He felt like he was flying on a skateboard, like it didn't really matter that his brain and his eyes couldn't agree about reading. He glanced at Mishti one more time. She was walking away with April and Delaney, and he sighed. Brandon was probably right; he probably wasn't ever going to be friends with Mishti or anyone like her.

After supper that night, Will sat at the kitchen table and tried to do his homework. Because of his dyslexia, he usually had less homework than most people. Or at least, he didn't have to read as much or write as much. That didn't mean he spent less time doing homework than other kids, though. For tonight, while everyone else was supposed to read a chapter out of the history book, Will had a shorter printout that talked about all the same things but with simpler words. Still, reading two pages had taken him nearly an hour, and he still wasn't sure what he had read. When he had to stop and figure out what a word was, he sometimes lost track of how the meaning of the word fit in with all the other words.

He was frustrated. Some of the kids in his class said he was cheating or being lazy. But even if his work was easier, he still couldn't do it.

Chloe, his seven-year-old sister, walked into the kitchen and opened the fridge, looking for a snack.

"Hey, Chloe," Will said. "Can you do me a favor?"

"What?" Chloe asked.

"Can you read this out loud to me?" He waved at the history papers. He hated asking Chloe for help. It made him feel stupid and embarrassed. But Chloe was a really good reader, and he was getting desperate to finish his homework.

"Okay." Chloe shut the fridge and smiled. Will thought she probably liked it when he had to ask her for help.

She read through the papers while Will listened. It took less than fifteen minutes, and he understood it all now.

He started to put the papers away so he could go watch TV, but then he thought about what his reading

teacher would say. Mr. Irizarry was a cool guy, even if he was kind of a pain sometimes. He put the papers down on the table again and sighed. He read them again, and this time it went a little faster. Because he already knew what the words said, he could put them together with the meaning more quickly.

The next day in school, Will's class had a substitute teacher. Substitutes made him nervous, because he never knew what they were going to want him to do. Ms. Currie was young and friendly, though—but then, just as Will started to relax, she opened the reading book and smiled at the class.

"Everybody open your books to the story on page 78," she said. "We're going to go around the room and take turns reading out loud."

What? Will's heart was suddenly pounding. He couldn't read in front of the class. He could barely read by himself. This was exactly the kind of thing that made him worry about substitutes.

Ms. Currie started with the row by the wall—Will's row—which meant he was going to be the fourth person to have to read. He was sweating now. He counted down to the paragraph he was going to have to read. It had three lines. But those were three lines too many, he thought. He tried to read the first few words before it was his turn, so he'd have a head start, but before he had even got past the second word, it was his turn.

"The boy," Will read. He had to figure out what came next, but it didn't help that everybody in the class was quiet, looking at him. He stumbled through the first line, not really sure what he was reading. He stopped again and tried to sound out the next word, but he knew he must be getting it wrong because people started to giggle. He felt his face get hotter and hotter. Sweat was sticking his hair to his forehead. Worse, tears started forming in his eyes, so that he could hardly even see the letters on the page anyway.

"Told you he was stupid," he heard April say.

He slammed the book shut and stood up. "Forget this! I hope you all think it's funny." He walked out of the class and slammed the door behind him.

He started crying as he walked down the hall. He didn't know where he was going to go at first, but then he turned around and walked toward Mr. Irizarry's room.

When Will walked in, the reading teacher was helping a younger kid with something, but he took one look at Will's face and told him to go sit down in the reading corner.

The reading corner had a couple of armchairs in it, with a little table between them. Will dropped into one of the armchairs, pulled his legs up, and put his head down on his knees. He stayed like that for a long time, as Mr. Irizarry talked to the younger kid. After a while, Will's breathing slowed down, and he stopped crying.

Eventually, the younger kid left, and Mr. Irizarry sat down in the chair across from Will. "Do you want to talk about it?"

"Not really," Will said, but he did. He lifted his head and looked at Mr. Irizarry. "It's not fair," he said. "Why can't I just learn like everyone else?" As he thought about it, he got even more frustrated. He told Mr. Irizarry about the substitute and having to read in class, about Mishti and wanting to be friends with her but knowing it would never happen.

"Wow," said Mr. Irizarry. "It's been a rough couple of days for you, hasn't it?"

"Am I ever going to get cured?" Will asked.

"Not cured, no," Mr. Irizarry said. "Your learning disability—dyslexia—is always going to be a part of your life. But you are going to overcome it. If you want to be an anthropologist, you certainly can."

Will felt a little better after he'd talked to Mr. Irizarry, but still not great. When he finally left the reading teacher's office, he discovered his class had gone to the library.

He walked into the library, hoping no one would notice him. Mishti, he saw, was reading a thick book with no pictures. Something like that would take him ten years to get through. Mishti glanced up and saw him looking at her. She gave him a tiny smile, but he was afraid she was feeling bad for him because he couldn't read. He wanted to smile back at her, but he was afraid, so instead he scowled.

After library, Will's class had music. Mr. Thomson, the music teacher wasn't in the room when everyone got there, so nobody sat down. Will went over to the piano and Brandon followed him.

"Hey, are you going to play something?" Brandon asked.

Will sat down at the piano and hit a few notes. He started to play a rock song he'd heard on the radio. He played quietly at first and then louder, pouring all his frustration about the day into the music.

"Woo hoo!" Brandon shouted and started dancing.

"Quiet!" somebody yelled, and Will realized Mr. Thomson had walked into the room.

He stopped playing and looked around. Other kids had been dancing too, and somebody was standing on a desk.

"Everyone sit down!" Mr. Thomson looked really annoyed.

Will started to stand up from the piano and then, because he liked that he'd made people happy for a change, he played one last flourish.

"Sit down, Will." Mr. Thomson wasn't yelling anymore, but he was looking even more angry. "Sit down at your desk and don't make me say it again."

Will sat down. The fun was over.

After school, Will took the bus to his dad's office at the university. This was something he did a couple of times a week. He loved his dad's office. It was full of interesting things, and, best of all, his dad was there. His parents had gotten divorced when he was only two, but he'd grown up spending afternoons with his dad on the university campus.

His dad was sitting behind his desk, typing something on the computer when Will walked in.

"Hey, Will! How was your day?"

"Lousy," Will said. "Pretty much the worst day of the year, I think."

"I have to go down to the museum to help set up a new exhibit," his dad said. "Why don't you tell me what happened on the way down."

His dad's department ran the museum, and Will loved it almost as much as his dad's office. His father listened to Will talk as they walked down the hall and rode the elevator down to the first floor.

"Mr. Irizarry is right," his dad said finally. "There are some things you can't do anything about and some things you can. You can't do anything about *having* a learning disability, but you can decide you aren't going to let it stop you from having a good life. You will learn to read. You will learn to read music, if that's what you want to do. No, it won't be easy, but most things that are worth doing aren't easy."

"Thanks, Dad," Will said, but he still felt worried. "What if I can't, though? What if I *never* learn to read?"

"Well," his dad said, "if you're really interested in something and really want to do it, you will. People find ways to overcome all kinds of challenges. And you aren't on your own, you know. You have people who care about you and want to help you succeed. There are technologies that will help you, too. I'm proud that you're my son. I love you, kid."

They had gotten to the museum, and Will pushed open the door. The first person he saw inside was Mishti. He stopped.

"What's wrong?" he dad asked.

"That's Mishti," Will whispered. He didn't want to go in anymore.

Mishti looked up and saw Will. She smiled at him and walked over. "Hi, Will," she said. "I'm sorry about earlier. April shouldn't have been so mean."

"Um, yeah," Will said. "What are you doing here?"

"My brother's going to school here," Mishti said, "so I asked him to take me to see the museum."

"We're going to set up a new exhibit," Will's dad said. "Would you like to help?"

"Oh, yes!" Mishti smiled at Will.

And suddenly Will felt a little better. Life wasn't easy, not with his learning disability—but maybe, like his dad said, the challenges were all worth it.

As he helped his dad open the display case, he looked over his shoulder and smiled back at Mishti.

Kids and Learning Disabilities

One out of seven people has some type of learning *disability*. A learning disability gets in the way a child learning new things, and often makes school more difficult in many ways. Some children with learning disabilities have trouble learning to read or solving basic math problems. Other kids with learning disabilities may have a hard time finishing the tasks they start or saying exactly what they mean.

A *disability* is a problem—either physical or mental—that gets in the way of a person doing what other people can do.

If something is *challenging*, it is hard to do. It makes you have to work hard to find a way to do it.

Since learning is so important to who we are and how we get along with others, learning disabilities can affect more than just school. At home, kids with learning disabilities might have a hard time following directions or getting along with brothers, sisters, or parents.

Though kids with learning disabilities may learn differently, they aren't any lazier or less intelligent than others. Learning disabilities can make learning *challenging*, but they don't make it impossible. With the right kind of help, kids with these challenges can be successful in and out of the classroom.

What Is a Learning Disability?

The term learning disability (often called "LD" for short) covers many different kinds of problems children can have with learning. Learning disabilities can get in the way of a kid's ability to read, write, understand math, speak, and listen. Some types of learning disability make it more difficult to follow directions, make decisions, or

A learning disability can affect a child's ability to learn the alphabet.

remember things clearly. Some children may have more than one type of learning disability.

A learning disability does not mean a child is not as smart as others. In fact, kids with LD are often as smart—or sometimes smarter—than their classmates. A learning disability is not a problem with intelligence. Learning disabilities are caused by differences

> When something is *processed* in your mind, it is understood and combined with all the other things you already know.

in parts of the brain that have to do with how information is taken in, *processed*, or communicated. Children and adults with learning disabilities have trouble processing the information they get from their senses because they see, hear, and understand things differently.

Signs of Learning Disabilities

Kids most often show the first signs of learning disabilities when they enter school. Parents may begin to notice that their child has trouble in certain subjects. Teachers might see that a student has trouble understanding some ideas or learning new material.

No one thing points to LD, but if a child has a few of the following signs he may have some type of learning disability. Kids who show many different signs may have more than one type of learning disability.

A child who has a learning disability may:

- have a hard time learning letters.
- learn language later than other kids.
- have trouble reading aloud.
- not understand what she is reading, or not be able to explain what she just read.
- not be able to spell correctly.
- have a hard time writing clearly.
- have a hard time using writing to express himself clearly.
- mix up certain words that sound the same.
- have fewer words in their vocabulary than other kids.
- get math symbols or numbers mixed up.
- not know how to start a homework assignment or project.
- not be able to follow directions.
- not understand some jokes or get why other people think something is funny.

In general, a learning disability is something that may get in the way of a child's reading, writing, speaking, listening, and math skills. If a child has problem in one or more of these areas of school, he may have some type of learning disability.

Types of Learning Disabilities

Many different disorders are called learning disabilities. "Dyslexia" is one of the most common learning disabilities. It's another word for a reading disability. Since so many school subjects require reading, this type of learning disability makes school very hard for those children who have it. Some kids may have more than one type of learning disability, as well. Here are a few of the most common types of LD:

- *Reading disabilities*: A reading disability (sometimes included in what's called a language disability) makes it more difficult for kids to learn to read and understand language. While reading, kids with reading disabilities may leave words out, mix up the order of words, or read words backward.
- *Writing disabilities*: Writing disabilities (which are sometimes also included in language disabilities) are often related to reading disabilities. A writing disability makes it harder for a kid to learn and understand the rules of language. Kids with writing disabilities may also have trouble using correct spelling and grammar.
- *Math disabilities*: Kids with math disabilities may have trouble learning to count or solve math problems. Some children with math disabilities may not be able

Learning disabilities can affect a child's ability to read, which can make school challenging.

to keep a number of objects or ideas in order in their minds.

Besides these types of learning disabilities, there are also learning disabilities that get in the way of:

- memory
- understanding expressions on people's faces and other *nonverbal* communication
- understanding spoken language
- understanding more than one step at a time in a set of directions
- making some movements or planning to make movements

Nonverbal has to do with something that is not put into words. For example, if you stomp your feet and slam the door, that could be a form of nonverbal communication that tells people you are angry.

Researchers are people who study things and do tests to try to figure out answers to questions. They are often scientists.

What Causes Learning Disabilities?

Though many doctors and *researchers* are working to find out the cause of learning disabilities, no one knows exactly what that cause may be. Doctors know that different parts of the brain control different actions or behaviors. One part of your brain, for example, understands what you see, while another processes language. If an area of a child's brain related to learning or understanding information doesn't work correctly, she may show signs of having a learning disability.

A student with a math disability may have trouble solving problems or memorizing facts.

Many different things can damage the way the brain processes information. If a child is hurt during birth, he may have trouble learning later in life, for example. Learning disabilities often run in families, a result of the *genes* children inherit from their parents. Infection in the brain can cause learning disabilities.

Genes *are tiny codes inside our cells that determine what we look like and what strengths and problems we have. These "codes" are passed along from parents to their children.*

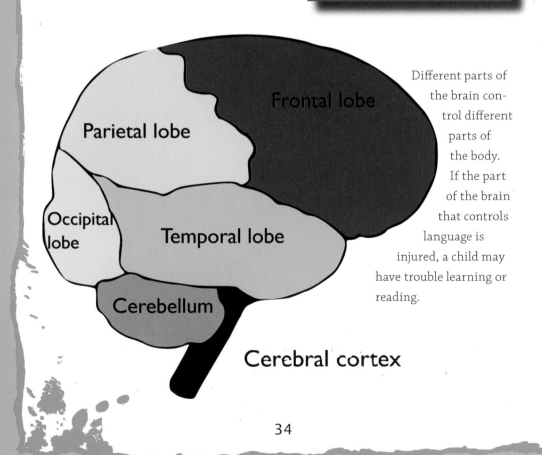

Parietal lobe

Frontal lobe

Occipital lobe

Temporal lobe

Cerebellum

Cerebral cortex

Different parts of the brain control different parts of the body. If the part of the brain that controls language is injured, a child may have trouble learning or reading.

Drug use by a pregnant mother can cause her child to be born with a learning disability, as well. Some accidents or injuries may also hurt the brain and make it harder for a child to learn.

Diagnosing Learning Disabilities

Most learning disabilities are *diagnosed* in schools. If teachers notice a child is showing signs of a learning disability, they may recommend that he should be tested for LD at the school. Parents who think that their child may have a learning disability may also ask that the school test their son or daughter.

The *school psychologist* will give the child special tests that will show the difference between how well she is doing in certain subjects in school and how well she

When something is *diagnosed*, a doctor or psychologist figures out what is wrong with someone and gives it a name.

A *school psychologist's* job in the school is to help diagnose and set up educational plans for kids who are having a hard time learning, for whatever reason. She may give tests to kids, spend time talking with them about their feelings and problems, and work with teachers to make sure that all kids with special needs are getting the education they need to do well.

could be doing based on her intelligence. Children may need to take more than one test for some types of learning disability. Once the testing is finished, the school psychologist will look at the test results to decide if the child shows signs of LD.

A child that is suspected of having a learning disability will undergo various tests to figure out why she is having trouble learning and to rule out other possible issues.

Doctors also check children who might have a learning disability for other problems that could be making learning more difficult. For example, children who are being tested for learning disabilities should also have their hearing and vision checked. If a kid isn't hearing or seeing instructions or assignments clearly, her troubles in school may not be related to LD. If a kid isn't hearing instructions or assignments clearly, her troubles in school may not be related to LD but to her hearing loss. If a student is *depressed* or *anxious*, he may not be able to do his best in the classroom, even though he doesn't have any form of learning problem.

> If a person is *depressed*, she feels sad very often, every day.
>
> If a person is *anxious*, he feels worried.

A child with a hearing disability might have trouble in school because he can't hear instructions correctly.

Diagnosing learning disabilities can be difficult because so many things can cause problems with learning.

Learning Disabilities and School

Most kids with learning disabilities can succeed in school with the right help. By making some changes in the class-

School may never be easy for a child with a learning disability, but with the right help she can overcome her challenge and succeed.

room, for instance, many kids can work around the challenges that LD presents. These changes are sometimes called accommodations.

Examples of accommodations include:

- giving students with LD more time to complete an assignment or test.
- letting a student who has trouble writing use a computer to type his work.
- giving both spoken and written instructions.

Children with learning disabilities will mostly do the same schoolwork as other kids their age. Often, changing the way an assignment is explained or the way a lesson is taught is enough to help kids with LD. Teachers can also work with students who need more one-on-one help in certain subjects.

Basic things like learning how to *organize* schoolwork or how to study for a test can also help kids with learning disabilities. Keeping things

> To **organize** something means to get it into order so you keep track of all the parts.

more organized can help a student with LD stay focused on completing assignments.

Here are a few other things that can help students with LD:

- Teachers may give students with learning disabilities breaks during longer assignments, lessons, or tests.
- Having recordings of lessons on CDs or tapes can be helpful to many kids with LD.

Though she might have a harder time in school, a child with a learning disability can be a great athlete or artist— and a great friend!

- Teachers can break up large projects or assignments into smaller pieces to make them easier to finish.
- Having tests read out loud to them and being allowed to tell their answers to someone who writes down the answers for them allows kids with learning disabilities to show how well they've learned the subject (whether it's science or social studies or some other topic). Otherwise, the test may only show how poorly they can read or write!

Learning Disabilities and Special Education

In the United States, around three million children with learning disabilities get *special education*. More than half of all kids in special education programs in U.S. schools have some type of learning disability. Not all kids who have a learning disability will need special education, but for many kids, special education will be the best way for them to succeed in school.

Special education focuses on the needs of each student. If a kid has a learning disability that affects her reading, she may work more on her reading in special education classes. If a writing disability

> *Special education* teaches kids who have trouble learning because of some disability.

is keeping a kid from succeeding in school, he may get extra help with expressing himself through words.

A law called the Individuals with Disabilities Education Act (IDEA) outlines how schools should decide which kids need special education. In order to *qualify* for special education under IDEA, the child's learning disability must get in the way of his learning new material, understanding schoolwork, or taking part in school activities. The IDEA law lists thirteen different kinds of disabilities that may mean a child will qualify for special education. Learning disability is one *category* under the law.

The IDEA law requires that:

> To *qualify* means to fit the definition of something or to meet the requirements.
>
> A *category* is a group or a certain kind of thing.
>
> When something is *evaluated*, it is examined to see in which category it belongs.

- the child has problems performing well at school activities.
- the child's parent, teacher, or other school staff person must ask that the child be examined for a disability.
- the child is *evaluated* to decide if she does indeed have a disability and to figure out what kind of special education she needs.

- a group of people, including the kid's parents, teachers, and a school psychologist, meets to decide on a plan for helping him. This plan is called an Individualized Education Program (IEP). The IEP spells out exactly what the child needs in order to succeed at school.

Succeeding with Learning Disabilities

Children with learning disabilities grow up to be adults with learning disabilities. Many of the challenges they experienced in childhood will continue all through their lives. Despite that, many individuals with learning disabilities become successful adults

> Someone who is *productive* earns money to support herself by doing things that help other people in some way.

who live happy, *productive* lives. A person with a learning disability may need to work harder than anyone else to reach a goal—but he CAN reach it! Many great athletes, artists, politicians, and movie stars had a hard time in school because of their learning disabilities—and yet they were able to grow up and accomplish great things.

Children with learning disabilities aren't lazy and they aren't dumb. If a kid has a learning disability, he simply thinks and learns differently from others. This means he will have to work harder. He will need to learn to cope with frustration. Many times, he will need to figure out new ways of doing things, all by himself. He will need to be able to understand what he can and can't do, and he will need to learn to speak up for himself.

You can make his job easier by respecting the way others learn, by treating everyone the way you would want to be treated if you were in the same situation.

Although kids with learning disabilities have trouble with schoolwork, they can be good at many other things. They can be good athletes, artists, or musicians. They can be fun to be with. They can be good friends. They are worth getting to know.

Further Reading

Fisher, G. and R. Cummings. *The Survival Guide for Kids with LD*. Minneapolis, Minn.: Free Spirit Publishing, 2002.

Gehret, J. *The Don't-Give-Up Kid and Learning Disabilities*. Fairport, N.Y.: Verbal Images Press, 2009.

Grant, D. *That's the Way I Think: Dyslexia and Dyspraxia Explained*. London, UK: David Fulton Publishers, 2005.

Hodge, D. *Lily and the Mixed-Up Letters*. Plattsburgh, N.Y.: Tundra Books, 2007.

Janover, C. *Josh: A Boy with Dyslexia*. Lincoln, Neb.: iUniverse, 2004.

Robb, D. B. *The Alphabet War: A Story About Dyslexia*. Morton Grove, Ill.: Albert Whitman & Company, 2004.

Silverstein, A., Silverstein, V. and L. S. Nunn. *Dyslexia*. New York: Scholastic, 2001.

Stern, J. and U. Ben-Ami. *Many Ways to Learn: Young People's Guide to Learning Disabilities*. Washington, D.C.: Magination Press, 2009.

Find Out More on the Internet

Council for Learning Disabilities
www.cldinternational.org

The International Dyslexia Association
www.interdys.org

LD OnLine
www.ldonline.org

Learning Disabilities Association of America
www.ldanatl.org

Learning Disabilities Worldwide, Inc.
www.ldworldwide.org

National Center for Learning Disabilities
www.ncld.org

National Dissemination Center for Children with Disabilities
(NICHCY)
www.nichcy.org

Disclaimer

The websites listed on this page were active at the time of publication. The publisher is not responsible for websites that have changed their address or discontinued operation since the date of publication. The publisher will review and update the websites upon each reprint.

Index

About the Authors

Sheila Stewart has written several dozen books for young people, both fiction and nonfiction, although she especially enjoys writing fiction. She has a master's degree in English and now works as a writer and editor. She lives with her two children in a house overflowing with books, in the Southern Tier of New York State.

Camden Flath is a writer living and working in Binghamton, New York. He has a degree in English and has written several books for young people. He is interested in current political, social, and economic issues and applies those interests to his writing.

About the Consultant

Dr. Carolyn Bridgemohan is board certified in developmental behavioral pediatrics and practices at the Developmental Medicine Center at Children's Hospital Boston. She is the director of the Autism Care Program and an assistant professor at Harvard Medical School. Her specialty areas are autism and other pervasive developmental disorders, developmental and learning problems, and developmental and behavioral pediatrics.